KARMA

CHOICES AND CONSEQUENCES

F I R S T   E D I T I O N
Published in 2019

Author: Randolph W. Mack

Website: www.RWMack.com

ISBN: 978-0-692-09624-6

Category: Marriage / Dating / Relationships / Divorce / Religion

Library of Congress Cataloging-in-Publication Data

Publishing Consultant: Leandrea Rivers Owens (laowens.com)

Editor: Barbara Joe (Amani Publishing LLC)

Proofreader: Kiera J. Northington (itsthewritestuff.com)

Photographer: Eric Bennett

Cover Designer: Barbara Upshaw-Mayers (Aura Graphics and Design)

Formatting Designer: Eli Blyden | CrunchTimeGraphics.com

Printed & Published in the United States of America

DEDICATION

This book is dedicated to my wife, Michelle, and kids;
Shiloh, Adonis, and Giavonnie.

I love all of you and it's because of you that I was inspired
to write this book.

I thank God for all of you and there's nothing
I would not do for any of you.

We're all we got!

KARMA

PREFACE

When a man truly evolves from simply being a self-seeking character into a soul that's seeking God, it is at that point he reaches his full potential. It is at that stage he realizes "he is the world and the fullness thereof." He understands this based on the reality that when he ceases to exist, so does the world itself. Although it may go on for others, it will no longer influence the outcome of his eternal fate. For a man to get to this level of spiritual thinking, he must be free from the physical distractions in this world such as self-gratification and the collection of material things that give him the perception of being self-sustaining. The man, who is blessed to come into the knowledge of this truth, knows internally that his time in this world is only allotted to him to acknowledge God to determine his eternal fate.

In Karma, you will be enlightened as you realize that although you live in this *physical* world, a parallel *spiritual* world exists. Being able to discern this will be the difference between *life* and *death* superseding your own physical death. *Choices, desires, destiny, love, and faith* are the driving forces behind this; it's the submission that there will be accountability to the Almighty Living God. You're invited to open your *heart* and *mind* to the poetic expressions contained in *Karma*.

TABLE OF CONTENTS

KARMA

CHOICES AND CONSEQUENCES

RANDOLPH W. MACK

Karma Part One

Hello, my name is **Karma**. My first warning to you is do *right,* or I'll come back with drama! I am the universal reinforcement of what you put out—you get back; the enforcer of what goes around comes around to repay you whether *wrong* or *right*. It all depends on what you do now to determine how I will treat you later. I can be *instant,* or I can come to repay you long after your transgressions are forgotten.

I can appear to be a blessing, but that's only to get you to let me in so I can teach my lesson. An example of this is how you may see me as a lover bringing joy. When in truth, it's me coming back to cause chaos to repay you for betraying someone else before.

If your deeds were indeed *good,* I could come back at a time that you may be in despair and bring *comfort* and *stability* when it seems no one else cares. I can come in many forms even the way I've come to you in this poem.

I'm known all over the world and even accepted by most religions if not by all. I can be the key to your rise or the force behind your fall.

Don't think you can deny me, and even if you try, I will laugh at your tears when you're crying. Why? I'm like a boomerang you throw and forget about, but when it's your time, I will turn around and seek you out.

Some call me *good* karma and some call me *bad*. Which karma I am depends on the things you have done—if I will make you *happy* or *sad*. You have no reason to fear me as long as you're doing right. But if you're doing wrong, I will return like *a thief in the night*.

No one is above me and can make me go away. I am **Karma** and could be the reason you live your last day. My message to you is to live a clean life and be true. Don't take me for granted because I will come back at any time out of the blue.

If you love me and respect me, too, God Almighty and I will protect and sustain you. You can even say I am a judge with *power* and *authority* from high above. When God says that "vengeance is mine," He's speaking of me, **Karma**, and I will deliver it to you when He chooses the time. It doesn't matter about your status or class. If you're doing wrong, I will have the last laugh!

In conclusion, so it will not be any confusion whether you acknowledge me or think I'm not even true … Just remember I'm **Karma,** and I will always find my way back to you!

Love

⬧

How would you know me if you met me? Would you be able to recognize me by the sound of my voice? If I touched you, would you, in turn, embrace me? If you knew I would be good to you and good for you, would you be willing to extend yourself and meet me in the middle? If I told you that to get me, you would have to give you, would you be willing to sacrifice yourself for me? Do you know what color I am, my size, my strengths, and if I have any weaknesses? If I told you I will be with you always, would you give me your forever? If I told you God had chosen me above all others, could you figure me out?

If I told you I was worth more than money and gold, would you treasure me? If I gave my word that I would carry you, would you be willing to walk with me? I can cause you to smile and cry, but through both, I will be with you. Do you know the reason why? It's because I'm loyal and true and will never forsake you.

I am patient. I am kind. I do not envy. I do not boast. I am not self-seeking. I am not easily angered. I keep no record of wrongs. I do not delight in evil but rather rejoice with the truth. If you let me, I will be your sunrise even when your sun sets. I will be your light even in the dark. I will be with you even when it's your time to part. In truth, I am a part of you now and have been from your start. You can even say I was sent to you from above. *Do you know me now?* I am Love!

Fragile

I have always considered myself strong enough to go through whatever I had to deal with in life. While feeling strong, I have had many moments of feeling frail. One time, which turned into several, was when I was involved in a relationship, where I thought the other person loved me as I loved her.

Only to find out my feelings were just that, mine! I felt betrayed to the extent that, to this day, I am reserved to ever trust anyone again. I question where I'm at now because of where I was then with my feelings. I had opened up myself and taken off my mask and showed my true face.

Since that experience, I am suspect about whether I am seeing the real faces or the faces they want me to see. It's weakening to have a woman look me in the face, sleep with me, eat with me, and say, "I love you" only to find out they are saying the same thing to someone else.

To trust again is, in itself, being fragile. Especially considering that I've had it done to me. Likewise, in my youth, and in error, I've done it to women myself. After deception on this level, is it possible to really know what women are capable of doing when it comes to love and lust? Anytime I've involved myself with women personally, I've been left in a state of being fragile because their actions caused me to go from feeling whole to feeling fragmented.

After getting past betrayal, I was left with is she being real? My answer, for now, is I don't know. I guess that's something only time will reveal!

Questions

When I think of religions, I 've come to realize that there are many. As I accept this, I am convinced that what others believe—they are as certain that what they believe is the truth as much as I do. Is it possible that there are many gods? Or do you believe the Scripture in James 2:19 that says, "You believe that there is one God; you doest well: the devils also believe, and tremble." I question if I will be worthy to receive God's promise of eternal salvation.

Will my faith and works be enough to receive His grace? I question why I am here in a place meant to be punishment for the devil and expected to do so many things for salvation or be faced with the prospect of falling short.

Keeping in mind Hebrews 10:31, which says, "It is a fearful thing to fall into the hands of the living God." Am I wrong for asking these questions knowing that Titus 3:9 says, "But avoid foolish questions and genealogies, and contentions, and strivings about the law, for they are unprofitable and vain." Every time I try to wrap my mind around the place God dwells, His majesty, His structure, vision, or foreknowledge, I realize that He is so expansive and far-reaching that my mind cannot grasp His fullness. I even question who I am.

Not the person called by a name, but my very soul, and if it's possible to reconcile my limited physical existence with my infinite soul. One thing I don't question is my love for God, who is my true first love. Although I have questions, I keep in mind 2 Corinthians 10:5, which says, "Casting down imaginations, and every high thing that exalteth itself against the knowledge of God, and bringing into captivity every thought to the obedience of Christ." With this, I do question, but I have no doubts that my Lord is faithful and true. Do you have any questions, or do you know all the answers?

Balance

Balance is essential its necessary to separate smiles from cries. Balance is something that is acquired through experience and longevity. From experience we become aware of what's good for us as opposed to what's good to us. From longevity we learn how to simplify our lives with a clear distinction of how what we need outweighs the things we may want. Balance by definition is a (condition in which different elements are equal).

In life we all face ups and downs and with some fortune and instinctive drive we accomplish goals and desires to balance the two. Without balance, setbacks from trial and errors could easily supersede our potential to be the best we can be. Without balance the death of a loved one could stagnate us from moving forward to live our own lives.

Without balance we could lose hope with love based on despair caused by someone who professed to love us.

Balance can be one of the most important virtues we can have to remain humble and acknowledge "A Higher Power" that will in turn produce a faith that we can have eternal life in paradise.

With balance we acquire the ability to become self-reliant and resilient enough to build even when it seems like everything around us has fallen apart. Proverbs 4:7 says "Wisdom is the principal thing; therefore get wisdom: and with all your getting get understanding. With understanding we are balanced enough to know all things are possible through our Lord who strengthens us...

Dig Deeper

My love, I'm giving you this poem out of necessity as well as a source of inspiration that will excel you to the apex of our love. I say necessity because my love for you cannot be contained within me. It's so powerful that it almost seems peculiar, meaning that in order to get *love,* you must give it; and once you get it, you have to give it back to keep it.

While love can go deep into one's very soul, it must be renewed *constantly* and *consistently.* It must be *affirmed* and *confirmed* by the recipient and the person transmitting it. This poem is entitled *Dig Deeper* because I am convinced that for every level of *love* reached, there's an equal amount to be received.

Love being infinite and having the potential to transcend all depths and distances, must be *pursued* rather than *assumed.* At the point when we feel we have given all that we can to show our love, that's when we must *push forward to reach the next level.*

This very determination is the same attribute that separates *challengers* from *champions.* One must have determination because of love's companion that is intricately entwined with it, which is pain. Some say joy is greater than pain, but in truth, they are inseparable. Wherever joy is, pain is there lying dormant and trying to invoke itself at the first chance given. And while we all try to avoid the latter, in reality, the deeper *sorrow* carves into our being, the more *joy* our hearts can contain the characteristics of God Himself, who is the essence of *love.*

So many people have their own interpretation and translation of what love is to them and what it *should, could,* and *would* do. But the best definition I have ever seen or heard of love is God's. This definition scintillates and illuminates through all darkness; it bridges the gap between *misunderstanding* and *clarity.* It provokes embracing while assuring forgiveness.

While I can say I have witnessed and even been involved in relationships that approached the standards set forth by God, I cannot say likewise that I've experienced its *true* depth nor height. One thing that is apparent to me is most of us approach relationships from the physical perspective.

When in truth, they should be established from a spiritual aspect. This can only be done through unwavering faith in God. *Faith* should be the key to secure all relationships and also the lock to sustain them.

Through faith, if we include God in our *love* and *life*, it will lead us to prosperity in our health and wealth. If faith is used as a base to build marriages on, their foundations will be strong enough to uphold whatever is placed on them or around them. I want to be clear—this is a plateau I am *striving* to reach and being enlightened, I believe this is a journey we should travel together. I have been praying to my Lord that He will strengthen us for this voyage in our pursuit of "the truth."

For me to reach "the truth," I want to fully reveal *my* truth. First, let me say that I love you without and beyond measure. You are and have been a source of *passion* and *pleasure* for me from the very beginning. I must admit I have not given you one hundred percent of myself. Not because you were not deserving of it, it was simply because I was not one hundred percent complete to be able to do so.

Acknowledging this, I want to thank you for carrying me when I did not walk with you. Thank you for being my constant companion, my confidant, my lover, and my friend. The patience and poise you have shown has far exceeded my expectations and is something that can only come from a woman with a calm and gentle spirit. For this, I will love you always and even forever. While I'm using this poem as a means to relay and profess my love to you, if I could, knowing you are worthy, I would have heaven and all of its angels recite it to you. I sincerely believe you are a distinguished guest from heaven itself; here but merely a moment to show me the way to eternal life.

Because of your love for me, I am convinced that Romans 8:38-39 is true. It says, "For I am convinced that neither death nor life, neither angels nor demons, neither the present nor the future, nor any powers, neither height nor depth, nor anything else in all creation will be able to separate us from the love of our God." One thing is for certain, and two things are for sure: From this point on, I will do everything I can to become acceptable in God's sight, and I will "dig deeper" to reach the next level of loving you.

The Clear Print

Sometimes we accept or take on the characteristics of our loved one, assuming it's the right thing to do at the time for the sake of love. But in truth, the bad we accept from others can become more than just a reflection of the other person; it can become our traits.

In all relationships, people pick up habits from each other. Some good and some bad. The important thing is to remain yourself while becoming a part of them; to remain yourself while they become a part of you. Most often when people in relationships want you to change, it's not because of you. It's because they want you to adjust to their own flaws. Because of this, I've found myself confronting the question of what's the difference between *love* and *feelings*?

Understanding love and how it transcends individual thoughts, I say if one can see them self doing something outside of the person they profess to love, then by definition "it's *not* love" but rather a consensual relationship that will end the same way the previous ones have. I think this is self-evident when considering how many relationships people get involved in before actually realizing there is a difference between *feelings* and *love*. Then they agree to pursue love and its infinite reach together. *Most* relationships start with excitement, hope, and thoughts of, "This is the one for me." In truth, they also start out with small lies that have the potential to become big and personal agendas that become priorities as well as the pursuit of self-gratification. By the time the latter is realized, they have already given all they have and then comes the question, why buy the glasses if we've drunk all the wine?

These things should all be apparent when considered that one of the most hurtful pains we have experienced has come from the hands of those who proclaimed to love us. The moral of this message is to love yourself, which will invoke self-imposed standards, self-respect, and self-sustaining stability. With this, you will be able to see who is not only on the same page with you, but also *in the same book*! Understand being on the same page could be in *two different* books.

What Makes A Man

$\diamond$

What is a *man*? What makes a *man*? Is a *man* a leader or a follower – or could he be one who knows when it may be time to do both? Is a man loud or silent – or is he one who can whisper and be heard by those near and far? Is a man one who goes fast or moves slow – or does a man believe that it's not how fast or slow he goes but rather how far he gets that matters?

Is a man rough or gentle – or is he capable of conflicting and comforting? Is a man an instigator of war – or does a man initiate peace? Will he know when one or the other is inevitable and know how to deal with it accordingly? Does being a man mean being a good husband to his wife, believing the adage that "Behind every successful man, there is a good woman" – or does a man know that his wife's place is not behind but rather beside him?

Does being a man mean to be simply a father to his kids – or does a man believe that in being a great father, his number one goal is to guide his children back to our Father in heaven, knowing they were God's children before they became his?

Does a man believe in God – or does a man feel he is his own *Alpha* and *Omega*? Does a man feel that he lives only by chance, but he chooses who and what he loves so he can determine his own destiny? What things are important to a man? Is it merely having peace of mind, financial stability, and a virtuous woman?

Can a man *ever* be satisfied – or will the more he gets, the more he will want? Can a man be defined by any of these things – or is what makes a man "*his* definition of himself?"

What makes you a man?

New Beginning

⬥

Each day is not merely a *new day*. It's also a *new beginning* to strive towards our goals and to fulfill them. Each new day presents the chance for us to refine and define ourselves; it gives us the chance to grow beyond measure and evolve into our visions. We know we can be the sunrise and sunset of each day by scintillating from within using our own light to illuminate the paths we create as we go forward.

With each new beginning, we should entwine with opportunity the desire to give our best as we trust in God to do the rest. When we reach our apex, it is at that point we become aware that God is not only the author of our life but also the finisher of our salvation. When we use each new beginning, it is essential that we acknowledge God in all aspects of our love as we seek stability in life.

As we proceed, our path is toward the truth as we inspire others around us to be witnesses to the truth that God is "the beginning and the end." If this is not a point you have reached in your journey through this life with your new beginning, I encourage you to *dig deep* within yourself as you continue your voyage to fulfill your *destiny*.

Go Forward

In this life, it is our destiny to *go forward*. In spite of adversities, we must push ahead! Despite facing obstacles, we must strive to reach our goals. Having a desire to *go forward* must become more than a wish. In action, it must become a way of life. All of the things we set out to accomplish must be based in reality and be within our potential to reach them.

With this, we should focus on the process of finishing rather than what it will take to even begin. In essence, we should see ourselves at the completion of our goals even as we begin to set them. In our lives, we will all face some trials and travesties. Some by chance and some through our choices, but being enlightened by them is the path we traverse to become mature adults and distinguishers of what's good to us versus what's good for us. Even being able to discern the truth, from a lie.

Going forward means letting go of hurt from others. Not because you are weak, but because you are strong! Strong enough to accept disappointment from others with the grace of an adult instead of with the grief of a child. Regardless of what we set out to do, we must realize that in life as we go forward, what counts is not how fast we go but rather how far we get. We must reach for success and stability not assuming it is something that will come to us without effort.

Going forward is an ability some inherit, and some evolve into. Regardless of how it's acquired, the drive to do so is the same in both, which is to hold on when others would let go. Going forward motivates us to lead rather than compromise and follow.

Being a leader invokes others around us to also give their best and the rest to fulfill their destiny and purpose. So be a star and always remember to shine, knowing your light could lead the way for others *to go forward!*

Alpha and Omega

My love, you are the first and only person I want to spend the rest of my life with. I feel like everything I've experienced up until this point was only a prelude of what was to come with you. Since you came into my life, I feel I know what the true essence of love encompasses. Because I value our relationship, I will not let anyone take your space or place! I came to this point after considering where I've been, where I'm at, and where I feel we have the potential to go. In truth, I only want to go where you are.

When I'm with you, regardless of where it's at, I feel like that's where I'm meant to be. When we are apart, I anticipate every moment of reuniting with you as if I'm waiting to exhale so every breath of me will be filled with you. Every moment apart seems like an eternity, but with you, it seems like time stops because nothing else matters.

Each day begins with you; and every night, I look forward to doing it again with you forever.

I am yours and only for you. I will remain faithful, true, and even sacred for you all the days of my life and give my deepest love to you. It is my true hope that you love me as well and that you, too, are willing to give me your all and all. If we give all that we have, then we will always be intricately entwined until we become one over time. Love me as I love you; embrace me as I touch you. Believe in me the way I trust in you. Be mine today and tomorrow even as I am yours forever!

Can I Trust You

C an I trust you with me? I need to know that you are willing to give me all of *you* for all of *me*. When I say all of me, I mean my *past, present,* and intentions for the *future*. In turn, are you ready to give me your all and all? I feel the first step toward this is to have a level of loyalty that transcends simply believing in it to using it as a format to live by. Loyalty requires so much and invokes the truth whether one is *absent* or *present* with us - the truth extends not only to me but also to yourself. From unfortunate experiences, I believe that every time I have been lied to, a piece of me died.

Regardless of how great or small a lie is, it can cause you to question everything about the person doing it and even cause you to question your own self-worth. With this, I have come to the point that I don't want to start something that will come to an end because of deception or lack of loyalty. I'm not interested in going fast. I'm more focused on how far we can get. I would rather remain alone than to be with someone and still feel lonely.

Just living, we can encounter some situations from chance that may cause us some setbacks. But the pain from love is based on a choice to be involved in it with someone outside ourselves. We must protect each other with the love we have been entrusted with from each other.

I want to be in love with you and with love in you. I have a desire to love and a real fear of being hurt by "professed love." I know that *trust* is based on acceptance, and in my heart, I trust you; and in my thoughts, I even love you. It is my true hope that you are in love with me as well, and we will continue to evolve through our faith in one God, one love, and one mind until we become one in time!

Consider Me

W ill you consider me? I am a man with goals and aspirations to live my life upright as I submit my will to the Most High God with hopes that I will spend eternity with my Lord. Consider my ability to lead and set standards that others will follow.

Consider that I am a man amongst men. Consider I have been smooth as silk and as rough as concrete. Consider I have experienced poverty and wealth. "Lord, forgive my trespasses." My hands have embraced my children, and these same hands have punished men! I have experienced smiles and cries.

I have witnessed death and the beginning of my sons' lives. Consider that I have experienced much and taking all this into account, consider when I tell you that I have not experienced anything that compares to the love of God—I'm telling you the truth.

Consider all the things I said I have experienced, seen, and done all shaped me into being the versatile man I am today. Without these things, I would still be prone to making some of the mistakes I made in my youth rather than learning from them.

But with them, I have come to the knowledge of the truth that God is not the author of confusion; He is the finisher of peace. Consider that I have searched the very depths of myself and through this process of (erudition), I know who I am, my purpose, where I've been and why, even more, where I'm going and what it will take for me to get there.

Last, consider I want to be in *love,* and I can discern it from lust.

Consider me a man, who would love to be in a *faithful* marriage, *best friends* with my wife. Her confidant, her reinforcement, and her protector, meaning the *love* she entrusted me would be protected with my own love by never betraying her.

Consider when I look at myself, I find me to be acceptable in my own sight. With that, my opinion far exceeds any comments that are not consistent with the way I perceive myself. Before you judge me, consider the choices I had to choose from may have dictated the decisions I made. Consider me; I don't want to be viewed as being different. Instead, I want to be accepted because I am the same ... Consider me!

If I Only Knew

If I only knew the sun rose each day just to make light for you; if I only knew you truly loved me, I would have dedicated my life to you. When I say, "If I only knew," it's not to make excuses for why I did not understand you. What I'm saying is forgive me and accept that I love you, too. My love, as I look back on my life, it's clear that while you have been my lover, you deserve to be my wife.

It's plain to see that we are truly meant to be. I feel this way with all my heart and again, forgive me for not recognizing your love from the start. The point where I am today is because of you. I'm grateful you did not let anything tear us apart, and I love you for keeping me in *your heart*. By example, you have shown me how to *live;* and for that, my heart I equally give. I want you to know you are very special to me; an angel is what I believe you to be. You are my alpha and omega love; and for you, I thank God above!

If I Could Go Back

If I could go back in time, I would be yours, and you would *still* be mine. Believe me when I say I love you; when I tell you this, I'm being true. As I look back, I realize I've made a lot of wrong choices that I should have gotten right. I can see these things clearly now because of your exhilarating light. It took a lot for me to get to this point. Sometimes it's hard to do right until it becomes something you want. When I pray, there are three things I ask for in my life: One, that I be forgiven of my sins; Two, that I be acceptable in God's sight; and three, that He will bless me with you as my wife.

If you will open up and let me come back in, all it will take is *your choice*. Listen to me, I love you, can't you hear it in my voice? This is not about me saying something to simply sound good. These are things I feel for you, and the things I would do for you; I promise—I would.

If it were easy to go back in time, I would be with you instead of wondering what would be my next line. But since I can't go back, I wish I could be with you now. If you're wondering what the difference would be, I would love all of you with everything I am and truly with all of me!

A Woman's Worth

---◆---

There are so many components to being a woman. Strengths, virtue, compassion, principals, values, passion, and love are just a few. Women are queens, matriarchs, mothers, and the very vessels to sustaining and renewing all life. It is a marvel and a mystery to me as to how women can lead children, be providers, producers, protectors, cooks, teachers, spouses, and mediators within a family.

All this while holding down jobs either in or outside their homes, only to do it with less effort and more precision over time. Women are often the spiritual guides of their families, and they become more refined in their faith that God can influence the outcome of all things. To witness a woman full of grace and elegance is beautiful. To hear an eloquent woman speak can be captivating and mesmerizing.

To be in the presence of a woman, who is beautiful inside and out, is indeed special. We should all praise women for their true value, which is beyond measure. Men in all their strengths and glory come from women. So it should be acceptable if implied that women, from the moment of conception, give men their strength. They nurture them and sacrifice themselves for them, which is the true essence of strength. A woman has poise and patience that can only come from a calm and gentle spirit. A spirit that evolves and scintillates.

A spirit that is a witness to the truth and invokes the truth from those around her. Proverbs 31:10 asks the question, "Who can find a virtuous woman? For her price is far above rubies." Being a woman encompasses many traits. Some are inherited; some are acquired. But all and all to be a woman, certain standards must be met but not exceeded. Women should be placed at the apex of all love and life!

Mother's Day

◇

Today is called "Mother's Day." If it were up to me, *every* day would be this way. I thank God He chose you to be my mother, and even if I could, I would not choose another. Just thinking of how my life began – you carried me for nine months and raised me to be a man.

You are the root and the beginning of my sunrise. From the beginning, I could see the love for me in your eyes. You have always pointed me in the right direction and with that always came *love* and *affection*. You picked me up when I was down; you protected me from all hurt, harm, or danger if you felt it was around.

When I think of the role you have played in my life, I pray that I will be blessed with a woman *like you* to become my wife. Because of you, I know right from wrong; because of you, I believe in God, and that keeps me strong!

Your message to all of us has been to seek God above because the only way we could truly understand *love* is to walk by faith and not by sight; to put Him first while we pursue His light. All I'm really trying to say is, "I love you, and that if it were not for you, I would not be who I am today." So, have a blessed day; have peace, be still, and remember I love you always, forever, and even until eternity—I will!

$\mathcal{I}$'m $\mathcal{W}$ith $\mathcal{Y}$ou $\mathcal{A}$lways

---

I want to remind you that I'm with you *always*. Not just physically but spiritually, too, and if you ever miss me, just listen to your heartbeat, and you will realize that's me inside of you. Believe me when I say, "I love you," and God is my witness when I tell you, "I'm being true."

I want to be with you in love and life. Once we're in heaven, our souls will reunite. I will be with you through the sunny days or rain, and I promise to keep loving you through *joy* and *pain*.

Please, understand that I am *in love* with you, and I am *with love* in you, too. I would do anything for us to stay together. With this, I hope you can clearly see that I love *all* of you with *everything* I have and truly with all of ME!

One Day at A Time

---◆---

Please, Lord, help me to live my life *one day at a time*. Please, help me to understand Your will so I can make it mine. I promise if You show me Your way I will submit to your will until my last day. I feel I can say that I have done all I wanted to do. Now, Lord, my only desire is to please You!

How beautiful it is to be able to talk to You. How beautiful it is to know Your love for me is *never* ending and is true. I believe You are the creator of the heavens and the universe. Thank you, Lord, for loving me first. Please, help me raise my children to know that You are real. I want them to know they can come to You about anything, no matter how they feel.

I know they were Yours before they ever became mine, and I have faith that You will reveal Yourself to them when it is time. Please, Lord, hear my prayer and remember Your promise that *You will never forsake me* and that You will always be there. Bless me, Father, and forgive me of my sins. I know better now, and I promise to never do them again. I will give You my all until I get it right. I will give You my heart, mind, and soul, and love You with all my might!

Without You, I cannot do anything but with You, all things are possible. My Lord, my Savior, and my King – *one day at a time* is my prayer to You. I love You, Lord, and thank You for loving me, too!

What Can I Give

✦

Tell me, Lord, what can I give to cleanse my sins and be blessed to live? I want to know what I can do to show my love for You is *faithful* and *true*. I'm willing to give any and everything, to be with You, my Lord, my Savior, and my King. As I search myself and all my possessions, I realize nothing I have can compare to Your words and their valuable lessons.

By studying Your word, I realize you are not impressed by *wealth;* the most important thing I can give You is myself. Please, accept me, Lord, to approach Your light; help me resist temptation, and give me the strength to fight back! I believe there's power in prayer, and I believe You when You say, "You'll never leave me, and You'll always be there."

If You search my heart, You will see this is how I truly feel. I believe this is not only my fate, but this is also Your will!

Destiny and Desire

To be in love with you and with love in you is not only my desire, but I feel it is also my destiny. Throughout my life, I've heard of soulmates, and up until this point, I always took it as being a simple saying or just another romantic cliché. But my desire to be with you has exceeded simply wanting.

I believe it is my destiny to be with you and pursue reaching the level of having one God, one love, and one mind until we become one over time. Alone I can be content; but with you, I feel complete. I'm not saying I am dependent on you, but I am saying you can depend on me. By that I mean, you can trust me. I will never betray you, and my loyalty will be toward you and the love you entrust me with.

I'm willing to commit myself to you and walk through life with you regardless of where it leads us; and if necessary, I will even carry you. Based on my belief that you are my destiny, I trust have reasoned and concluded that together, we could be self-sustaining, and my love for you is without measure. In essence, I'm willing to give you all of me for all of you. I will not withhold anything from you.

I will love you always, forever, and even until eternity. This declaration to you is not merely a truth; it is the truth. I love you with all that I am, even beyond desire, reaching the point that I believe it is my destiny!

My Lord, Can You Hear Me

---◆---

Lord, can You hear me when I pray? If You do, then You know I do it every day! I pray knowing You loved me first, which is special knowing You are the creator of heaven and earth. There were times my faith in You was probably the shakiest, wondering if You heard my prayers? I almost became an atheist, but I always found a way to push ahead! Every time I remembered Your words and what they said.

As I look back, it's plain to see not only do my prayers reach You, but You are with me. Such as the poem *Footprints in the Sand*, You indeed "carried me when I was too tired to walk." This I now understand, I will never doubt You again. Embrace me with Your light and bless me with Your Holy Spirit to continue to lead me always from what's wrong to doing what's right.

Thank you, my Lord, for lifting me up every time I slip, trip, or fall, and I vow this day to give You my *all* and *all*.

The Voices of Angels

When I first heard them, they sounded like *the voices of angels*. But it seemed as if I'd heard them before. Their voices were so familiar; it was something I simply could not ignore. Therefore, I prayed and asked God had He heard them before?

He answered, "Yes," and said, "they were the voices of angels for sure."

I asked, "Were they guardians to watch over me?"

He replied, "Your relationship with them is a special one. In time, you will clearly see."

There were times I felt sad and even depressed, but every time I heard these voices, they caused my spirit to rest. These voices would take my happiness to another level and to hear them—there's no distance I would not travel. I often found myself reaching out to hear these sounds. This was when I realized every time I heard them, my children were around. Then it finally dawned on me what God had shared with me. In time, I would clearly see that I did have a special relationship with these voices. In fact, they were a part of me.

These voices were not only the voices of angels that I could now tell; they were actually the *voices of my children, and* that is why I knew them so well!

Heaven

C an you imagine being in heaven, and the things you would see? A place where even flowers sing praises to God all the time. A place where you could see angels with your eyes and not just in your mind. A place where you can see waterfalls of gold and sit and talk with Moses, Abraham, Israel, and other prophets of old. A place where when it rains you never get wet by a drop because the halo over your head, makes sure it stops.

A place where rain is not needed for thirst, but so it will produce a rainbow to remind us of God's promise to never again flood the earth. I can only imagine this will be a place like no other. This is the place that I will again be able to see my mother, father, and brother.

Can you imagine sitting with God one-on-one and Him pointing, saying, "This is the One who gave His life for you!" My only begotten Son.

There, you will see Him sitting on His majestic throne with angels all around him saying, "This is the Chosen One, whom sins of the world were placed upon." Imagine seeing the living God, whose love for us never wavered. Imagine seeing the One who never committed any sin and endured being crucified to unite us back to our Father again. Imagine seeing our Lord, our King, and our Savior.

Imagine a place with no sickness or bad health and no need for money because love will be your *true wealth*. Yes, heaven is truly a beautiful place. I am determined to see the only true God, and from within is where my mission will start. I hope that you, too, can imagine this vision of mine and that the stairway to heaven will also be easy for you to climb. So even though we may be separated by space and time, I'll see you in paradise as long as we have *one God, one faith,* one love, and one mind!

Crossroads

---◇---

In living we encounter many crossroads. Some of those roads can lead to changes in direction. Some can lead us to cross paths with someone that may become a part of our most intimate life. Some can even end up being dead ends. I've thought about how many times I've found myself being at a crossroad and how I got there.

Some of the crossroads I felt I needed to create because from self-evaluating I knew if I didn't have a change of course that I would be on a path that led to nowhere but despair and regret. Some of the crossroads I was led to by others and some I ended up on because I didn't listen to the advice of some who were warning me they had already been down the road I was going down and it led to nowhere. I came to a crossroad when I had to deal with the death of one of my beloved family members.

It's a feeling that caused me much grief but strengthened my faith in God in that all things work together for the good for those that love our Lord and are called accordingly to his purpose. Some of my roads were crooked, some had turns and some were straight. Some I traveled I feel were part of my fate. I'm not sure if I missed some roads where I should have made turns, I'm just thankful to be still on the crossroad where I can live and learn. Every day we are on a road that leads to some direction. The one I'm on now is the straight and narrow praying each step of the way for God's protection.

As I move forward I realize that it's roads all around me that I could take but I stay focused and calculated with precision so I won't end up on a road that ends up being a mistake. While we all have roads we will traverse, some can make our lives better and some can make it worse. The important thing is to be careful which one's you take because all roads don't lead to second chances and could lead to your family gathering at your wake!

Color Me You

I have experienced racism as a people, on the whole, and individually, as a person. The result and outcome being something that maybe God has reasoned with and know the benefits of it and how it outweighs the liability. I say, "Maybe my Lord has pondered it because He knows we are one, although we see ourselves as many. Even though the differences may be immense in the eyes of men, they are, in truth, minute.

I have been amazed and saddened by my personal experience with discrimination. I have sought to know how can a man, who claims to love the same God as me, hate me for no reason other than a label of color or race? I have tried to get past these thoughts and questions, but the issues are ever before me. I have sought after love only to be pursued by hate! I have been on time only to be told I'm late.

I have planted roses in some gardens only to see thorns grow. I've tried to embrace some who said right or wrong, NO! I really can't get to the root of why some feel this way. Truthfully, I don't think I will until judgment day; but for the present, I'm not stagnated by the *past,* and I have true *hope* for the future. I could adapt the notion of "an eye for an eye," but racism transcends individual implications and can result in universal ramifications.

It's astonishing how an isolated incident can *divide* a people. I can only wonder if the division was inherited or simply ignorance by *choice* or *force.* I think the biggest trick the devil has ever played was *the race game.* After that, heaven is here on earth if you have *fortune* or *fame.* Some say, "It's a thin line between love and hate," but in truth, the line is merely *a choice you make*! Please, choose wisely because it could determine your fate – with that, choose *love,* which will always bridge the gap between assumed differences. In turn, I hope *love will bridge the gap between you and me!*

Karma Part Two

Don't be surprised; I told you I would be back for you. I'm not sure why you didn't believe me the first time when I said I would be back when it was time, but I will be sure to make you see that I am real and erase all remaining doubt from your mind.

I thought from my last visit with you that you would have been more careful when choosing wrong or right, knowing you can't escape me because I work all day and throughout the night.

So, let's get to business, so I can repay you for all you have done when you thought no one knew, but I saw everything you did when you were not being faithful and true.

Now you may be saying why won't I just leave you alone, but you started again when you thought I was gone.

Well, answer me, what do you think I should do? Should I punish you, require your life, or let you explain why I should spare you? Before you speak, know the outcome has already been determined for you, not because of me but because of the things you chose to do.

As I told you before, I have two sides to me, and your choices will determine which side of me you will see. There's no need to start calling out to God saying, "Please, don't let this be!" Because in case you forgot, He is the One who sent me!

I told you no one could escape me, and I should not be taken for a joke. Ask death; I even made it have a stroke! I truly hope if you make it past me this time, you will consider me before you step out of line. Trust me; I get no pleasure in coming to you this way. But, as I told you in Part I, "I could return like a thief in the night on any given day."

Before I go, I want you to remember you reap what you sow. So do the right thing, and hopefully, if I see you again, it will be joy that I will bring.

ACKNOWLEDGEMENTS

To my brother and sisters:

I love you all and I know Mom would be pleased with all

of us for the lives we are living.

T. Man, Gina and Shelia;

it is my true hope that our Lord will be with you all,

now and even forever.

KARMA

SPECIAL THANKS

A very special thanks to my publishing consultant, Mrs. LeAndrea Rivers Owens a.k.a. L.A. Owens and her husband, Mr. Tony Owens special thanks. Thank you both for believing in me when no one else did. From the beginning, Mrs. Owens, your will to see this book become successful has been unwavering.

There were times I wanted to give up, but your encouragement pushed me ahead. What I thought was my limit was only the beginning of my threshold when it came to my determination to finish this book, thanks to you! Thank you Tony, for critiquing the poems. Mrs. Owens, not only did you help me get this book published with all your resources and contacts but your own books - *Dare I Express It: Volumes 1 & II* inspired me to write some of these poems. Thank you both for all the help and guidance. I'm thankful to you both.

KARMA

About the Author

I've often been told I have three last names, Randolph Warren Mack. I feel blessed to say that I have lived 52 years of life's experiences and look forward to a lifetime more. Currently, I reside in the "Sunshine State," a rare Floridian indeed.

I have 3 wonderful sons; Shiloh 17, Adonis 16 and Giavonnie 10. My lovely wife, Michelle was extremely instrumental in helping me get this book published. I was inspired to write by my cousin, Alphonso Pinkney who wrote several books while being a sociologist and long-term chairman of the Department Of Sociology at Hunter College in New York.

As a youth while visiting my grandmother's home every Sunday after church for Sunday dinner, my brother, sisters and I were basically restricted to what was called "the T.V. room" where our options were to read a book or sit and watch wrestling with my grandfather. I would always pick up one of Alphonso's books and was fascinated by his writings.

As I got older I got back into reading which eventually led me to start writing. By the time I realized it I had written 5 books, a series of children's books and over 50 poems. This book "Karma, is a collection of some of the poems that

I hope will inspire and even open the door to a new kind of poetic expressions.

I give you my assurance that by purchasing my book you will find it to be unique, relatable and stimulating.

It is my hope that you enjoy this read and get substance from the book. I promise there is more to come!

www.ingramcontent.com/pod-product-compliance
Lightning Source LLC
Chambersburg PA
CBHW071423040426

42445CB00012BA/1266